HOW TO MAKE PEOPLE LIKE YOU AND DO WHAT YOU WANT

The Miracle Formula for Magnetic Charisma, Making People Laugh, and Exerting Influence

I0521735

Richard Banks

Thank You!

Thank you for your purchase.

I am dedicated to making the most enriching and informational content. I hope it meets your expectations and you gain a lot from it.

Your comments and feedback are important to me because they help me to provide the best material possible. So, if you have any questions or concerns, please email me at richardbanks.books@gmail.com.

Again, thank you for your purchase.

INTRODUCTION

In our daily lives, we meet and greet thousands of people—and a few thousand of these people regularly come and go in our lives. Some are just passers-by who happen to cross our path, while others make a strong impact on us. It's as if they craft an instant impression on our mind and heart—a quick memory woven into the fabric of our being. These people don't need to do too much or talk too much to stand out. They mesmerize and charm whoever they meet.

They can steal the light from anyone—no matter who they are. You can find such people everywhere around you, and chances are you were thinking of a few names as you read the last few lines. These people aren't celebrities or necessarily famous, but there's something about them that fascinates people. They can sway people's thinking and convince them with the slightest of expressions and minimal words.

Whether they're just strutting down the street, delivering a passionate speech in a room full of executives, talking to a colleague at the coffee shop, or sitting quietly in a boisterous swarm of people, there's something about them that sets them apart. It doesn't take them long to make friends with those around them because their magnetic and charismatic appeal pulls in and delights anyone who comes in contact with them.

When a person develops control over how people around them react to their words and actions, they can maneuver and manipulate their way through many situations. The slightest bit of confidence and amiability can get you through a ton of challenges in life. So, it doesn't come as a surprise that people who have well-developed social skills, leadership qualities, confidence, and tactics for dealing with people are always on the upswing in both their professional careers and personal lives.

Who doesn't want to be such a person? A person who walks into the room and everyone turns to look at them, a person who's the life of the party, a person who says a lot with just a few words, a person who's invited to every social gathering, a person who can gather a crowd around them regardless of where they are, a person who can keep their cool even when the situation tenses up, a person who can be humorous, a person who's adored by many and always consulted for advice, a person who's always the priority for anything and everything.

Their hands don't go clammy when they're thrust into an unfamiliar situation, their heart doesn't run wild when they're called upon to speak, their tongues don't become tied when their words are met with criticism or snide remarks, they're not interrupted by anyone in the group, they aren't the last to get picked for a team or the final choice for a promotion, and they aren't afraid to strike up a conversation with a complete stranger.

9

Do you wish to be such a person? Then you must begin by cultivating certain qualities. Developing this set of qualities will require practice and breaking the chain of your old habits. You'll need to work on yourself day and night to be a better version of yourself who isn't afraid to make mistakes.

People start to develop personality traits from an early age. Children are commonly referred to as sponges because they pick up everything that's happening around them. They might reproduce the personality traits or characteristics of their parents, siblings, friends, or even characters in cartoons they watch or books they read. These traits are practiced repeatedly by the child until they're hardwired into the child's brain and become habits. If they become accustomed to being in isolation, that's also something they'll be more comfortable doing later in life.

With most people, habits are unconscious. They don't think before they perform a particular action; they just do it. It's like breathing: You don't think about breathing. You just breathe. Similarly, you don't think about creating or acting from habit. You're so accustomed to doing something that the action is unconscious.

If you want to be a better version of yourself—one who has significantly higher social capital, is a better leader, and is great at relationships, outgoing, fully confident, and has a lot of friends—you'll need to break the cycle of your current habits to make space for new ones. You won't only achieve your goals of becoming more social and charismatic, but you'll also develop qualities that will ensure prosperity in your relationships and work.

In this book, we'll discuss the myriad of qualities you need to make part of your personality, and we'll explore the process of how to do this. We'll discuss the day-to-day situations that all of us face and how to respond to them. We'll share tips, tricks, and activities to ensure that newer, better traits replace your habits.

First of all, we'll conduct an in-depth personality analysis. You can't begin to change yourself and your habits if you don't know what they are. By answering a set of questions, you'll start to gain a better understanding of yourself. Self-knowledge is the hurdle between you and your best self—which is inherently charismatic and magnetic. So, take out a journal or a piece of paper and answer the following questions:

- If I were to describe myself in three words, what would those words be?

- What are my goals/aspirations?

- What does my ideal life look like?

- What brings me absolute joy and satisfaction?

- What are the things that make me unique?

- What do I consider to be my strengths?

- What do I consider to be my weaknesses?

- What fears are holding me back?

- What are my most recurring emotions?

- What do I value most about myself and the world around me?

- How do others view me?

- What do others value most about me?

- Am I offering substantial value to those connected to me in my work, or do I have more to bring to the table?

Once you pinpoint what situations and traits are challenging to you and why, you'll know what shortcomings have arisen in your journey to becoming a magnetic individual.

You'll need the answers to these questions to decide the best approach for changing your habits. This approach includes how to hone your social skills, how to build stronger relationships, how to work on yourself, how to build your self-esteem, how to be more confident, how to read people and their body language, how to become more popular, and how to become a better listener, among other things. We'll also talk about developing a strong presence, making brilliant first expressions, small talk, body language, correspondence and hand movements, words and their impact, and how to be a more influential person in general. You can expect to learn about how to control and handle anxiety, stress, and pressure. You can also expect to learn a few tricks about time management and building habits from the ground up.

Before we begin, here's a word of encouragement: Don't give up. A lot of people have been exactly where you are now. Some have given up and gone back to being completely invisible, living in the shadows of those around them. Others have taken this journey as a challenge and cast themselves in the brightest of colors, setting themselves apart from everyone.

Here's your chance to hand-pick a vibrant color for yourself and wear it ferociously so that you, too, can become a leader among your peers. You'll no longer be a bystander; your walk will cause those around you to gravitate toward you. I can assure you that by the end of this book, you'll have a plethora of tricks up your sleeve that will aid you in making more friends and achieving all your goals. However, the key thing here is practicing the strategies, being consistent, and not giving up. You need to strengthen your willpower. You can do so by constantly setting reminders for yourself, whether about practicing a new quality or making time to relax. Create reminders around the house—whether this be by using a clock, alarm on your laptop, or even on your refrigerator. Write down what you want to practice on a piece of paper and stick it to the mirror in your bathroom, the closet of your bedroom, or the steering wheel of your car. The point is to place your reminders where you'll see them often.

On this journey, you'll make mistakes and falter along the way. But the key to success is to get up, dust yourself off, and keep going. You never know if victory is just around the corner! Yes, you'll embarrass yourself at times. Yes, you won't achieve gold on your first attempt, but you'll eventually get there. These techniques are proven to give you an edge on those around you. So, what are you waiting for? Your new life—full of friends, family, relationships, happiness, and success—awaits you! Embrace it with open arms!

Without further ado, let's jump into the first chapter, where we'll explore the importance of social connections! Happy reading!

CHAPTER 1 – THE IMPORTANCE OF SOCIAL CONNECTIONS

"Man is by nature a social animal." - Aristotle

Due to the nature of today's society, most of our day-to-day activities require that we be interactive. They require us to connect with those around us and make friends. Humans weren't created to remain isolated like islands. There's evidence of this from the earliest of times. Early societies traveled in groups—not only because of the power in numbers but also because activities like hunting, setting up a shelter, and other tasks were made easier through a cooperative effort.

17

Moreover, from the day a child is born, it develops connections and relationships with those around it. It's hardwired to connect with people and becomes profoundly social from a young age. We're drawn to those who help us, admire us, lead us, and take an interest in us. The impact of your first relationships reverberates throughout your life. If children are loved and taken care of from birth, they learn how to develop strong connections with others and thus are more likely to continue this pattern throughout life.

We're inherently, biologically, cognitively, physically, and spiritually social creatures. There's no denying that. However, in the world we live in today, interacting with others and maintaining social connections can be challenging due to a variety of factors. Anxiety, stress, depression, and low self-esteem are a few leading contributors; they prevent people from putting themselves out there. If you answered the previous set of questions, you should be able to identify what holds you back when it comes to having valuable social connections.

Many people tend to isolate themselves or avoid social contact without weighing the negatives of doing so. Social connection is as essential for the health of the human body as eating a balanced diet, getting enough sleep, or exercising regularly. When you interact with those that bring joy and peace into your life, your brain releases feel-good hormones like dopamine and oxytocin, which instantly improve your mood and elevate the state of your brain and body. Certain hormones remove tension from your muscles and create a sense of well-being.

While it's true that social engagement helps improve a person's emotional, physical, and mental health, it's also true that the lack of positive social involvement can have detrimental effects. Hence, one should always focus on the quality of their friendships rather than the quantity. For example, if you wanted someone in your life that you can rely on or celebrate with, you wouldn't call the person you talked to once at a conference; you're likely to call a close friend. That's the very essence of social connections. It's the sense of closeness or belonging you feel with an individual or a group of people. A study conducted by Pavey,

Greitemeyer, and Sparks in 2011 proved through strong scientific evidence that social connection is one of the core psychological needs of any individual.

Happiness is contagious; it spreads through social connections. The positive attitude of the company you keep will rub off on you.

Social Connectedness

Social connectedness can be divided into three core categories. You can sort your relationships using these categories to understand where you stand with each of your relationships. You can also use this process as a resource to elicit other people's opinions of you to see where you stand in their book. What you discover might exceed your expectations or fall short of them. Nevertheless, amicably ask someone the reason for their opinion, and reevaluate your stance. Think about what type of relationship you want to have with them, and then make efforts toward that end. Don't feel dejected if people don't seem to appreciate you. This just means you have to start learning more about yourself, and the beginning is always the hardest.

The three core branches of social connectedness are:

Collective Connectedness

In this dimension of social interaction, you're part of a group or collective. You don't stand alone as an individual in this type of relationship but are a member of a group of people. This is the relationship you're most likely to have as part of a strong family, support group, community, or a particular club/society.

Intimate Connectedness

This is the degree of connectedness you have with a special someone in your life. You can feel this with a close friend, a partner or spouse, or anyone who loves you, accepts you, cares for you, and supports you just as you are.

Relational Connectedness

This dimension refers to interactions that are mutually rewarding. You can have this with your colleagues at work, in a partnership, or in a team project.

The most treasured social connections are with those who are genuinely concerned about your happiness and well-being. They inspire you, support you, and make you feel less stressed or burdened. These connections are meaningful and beneficial.

What Do People Look for in Friendships?

Here are a few key factors that people look for when seeking meaningful and gratifying friendships.

Trust

People with whom you share a strong bond feel comfortable enough to give you their honest opinion and offer constructive criticism. They aren't afraid to hurt your feelings. If you don't know someone well, they'd be reluctant to offend, so either their opinion will likely be sugar-coated or disingenuous. Accurate advice can only be gained from those who trust you and vice versa.

Respect

Respect is a broad term that includes everything from respect of another person's boundaries and values to respect for you as a person—what you stand for, what you do, what you believe in, and respect for those around you. Without the presence of respect, no relationship can work.

Acceptance

Those with whom you have a genuine friendship or relationship accept you. They don't try to negate you or ask you to change things about yourself that constitute who you essentially are. They welcome you as you are. They provide you with companionship that makes you feel more socially accepted in a larger group. When they accept you, you begin to discover common ground and become more comfortable with them.

Unconditional Support

The support provided by genuine relationships shouldn't come at a cost. It shouldn't be based on bargaining: "If I'm doing this for you, you have to do that for me." Rather, it should be, "You need help, so I'm here." No hesitation, just support without any conditions. Support helps you feel less lonely. You have people with you in your best times and your worst times. You're motivated by these people to do better and be better. When you're caught in a pickle, you can turn to them without thinking twice.

Obstacles to Healthy Relationships

There are a ton of factors that hinder people in developing stronger relationships. These include the stress and anxiety of approaching someone we don't know, the presence of cliques, the distractions of social media, working 24/7, not valuing other people enough, and much more. The lack of social connection can isolate a person from the rest of the world. When a person is alone, they're likely to become consumed by their thoughts and overthink everything. Overthinking is a key trigger for negative thoughts to brew.

Negative thoughts translate into negative actions and exuding a negative vibe. People tend to distance themselves from those who are negative and pessimistic. Being a victim of your mind will also make your self-esteem plummet. You won't feel enthusiastic about anything. The tiniest change around you can send you into a downward spiral. Your judgment will be clouded, and you'll make skewed decisions that will impact your personal and professional life.

Suffering defeats left and right takes a toll on our physical health. People who feel isolated often find unhealthy coping mechanisms to fill the void when social connections collapse. These might include overeating or overspending to get a temporary high or alcohol or substance abuse.

Social connection keeps a person grounded. It keeps them in touch with reality. They're aware of what's happening around them. They can make valuable connections that can help them climb the ladder of professional or personal success. Being connected socially pushes them to be a better version of themselves. We tend to have a positive outlook on life when we're surrounded by positive people.

The Benefits of Strong Social Connections

Much like our relationship with ourselves, good relationships with others are conducive to happiness and fulfillment, providing meaning and purpose in our

25

lives. When you have positive relationships, you inundate your life with love and admiration, and you feel better about yourself. You feel worthy, valuable, and that you belong. A person who feels good about themselves brews positivity. They maintain a positive outlook on life and are ready for any challenge that life throws at them, which means they're prepared to face anything. Having strong relationships also gives you a sense of security. It's like a cushion you can always fall back on—a cushion of unconditional support and love.

Physical Health

Just as exercising can benefit your physical health, so can spending time with those you love. Positive social connections can help reduce stress and increase cardiovascular health. Additionally, studies have shown that social interactions can lead to a more robust immune system.

Mental Health

Interacting frequently with others improves your cognitive functions. Your brain becomes sharper. The more you hang out with someone, the more characteristics you can identify about them. You understand how they deal with people, react in different situations, and handle life in general. Participating in social activities can also help your mental health by reducing depression and anxiety. It can lighten your mood and make you feel happier. Additionally, suicide, mental illness, and alcoholism rates are much lower in people who feel a sense of belonging.

How to Improve Your Social Skills

We've talked about numerous benefits that come with social interactions. Surely this must have enticed you to improve your social skills and increase your social status. Remember, merely improving your social skills isn't the point; cultivating relationships and stronger friendships is also essential.

Face-to-face Interactions:

Building connections and working on them requires time, effort, and consistency. If you want to create a strong relationship with someone, don't give up. Notice what they're communicating between the lines. Take an interest in them, listen closely, and ask follow-up questions. Don't ignore this advice. If you don't take an interest in their life, they won't take an interest in your life. But always know when to stop pushing. Ask them if they want to talk about something. Be genuinely concerned. Reciprocate the confidences they share with you. Make small gestures. Small steps can lead to extraordinary results.

Find the Courage to Talk to People

Meeting a group of people you don't know can be intimidating. Crowds can be frightening. But remember: with great risk comes great reward. If you ingratiate yourself with someone who's part of a group, you potentially can make multiple friends instead of just one. Start by approaching someone who's standing or sitting alone. Walk over to them, and ask them if they need anything. Introduce yourself. Smile. Hold your hand out. Tell them something unique. See if they're interested. Usually, meeting people with whom you share mutual friends is easier.

Don't settle into the comfort that comes from being alone. Branch out and interact. It will take courage, but remember, this is true of everyone. We all need courage to interact, and this isn't something you can buy on the Internet. You muster it from inside you. You don't have to try to do this all at once. Take small steps. Start at the grocery store. Offer to help someone carry their groceries. Get something they can't reach from an upper shelf. Give them a smile. Let the person behind you in the checkout line go in front of you.

Before you arrive at a party or gathering, do some research. What kind of people will be there? What do these people usually talk about? Learn about these topics and use them as fuel for conversations. Meet a friend or two before going to the party. Your friend can probably introduce you to more people. Call on one of your family members before you attend a family engagement and discuss what's happening in their life. This is, again, fuel for conversation.

Be Mindful and Accepting of People

When you meet someone new, you won't instantly know who they are, their views, and their values. If they're fully to the right on the political spectrum, and you're fully to the left, don't assume you have nothing to talk about and walk away. Listen to what they have to say. Give them time to open up. Keep an open mind. Don't judge their opinions or belittle what they say, even if your views are totally different. Be open to other schools of thought and engage in conversation, no matter how polarizing it is. People come in all shapes and ideologies. Accept them as they are. Please don't pick them apart. We all have flaws, and we all have unique backgrounds and personalities.

We have a habit of judging people and situations. We develop perceptions before we even meet a person or encounter a situation that dictates how we think and behave. This can twist the entire outcome. So, keep an open mind. Don't develop a perception beforehand. Give people a chance. They might surprise you. Maybe after you get to know someone better, they turn out to be amazing. When you accept them as they are, they'll accept you as you are. Don't close the door to potential friends.

Share Yourself

Opening up to others is even more difficult than meeting new people. When you open up to someone, you share intimate details about yourself and your life.

This makes you feel vulnerable, and that's uncomfortable. None of us likes to cast ourselves in a dark light. None of us wants to share our weaknesses, flaws, and things we feel insecure about. So, sharing your stories with people can be especially hard. This is exacerbated by the fact that you don't know how the other person might react. They might be understanding and sympathetic, or they might just brush off whatever you've told them. They might respect you and your story and keep it to themselves, or they might gossip about it with someone.

One of the most effective tools to connect with others is storytelling. When you meet someone new, say less and ask more. Ask them about their life and their opinions. The other person will feel valued and sense you're interested in getting to know them. This sets a solid foundation for a strong friendship. However, don't just interview them about themselves. It would help if you shared your stories, too. Sharing yourself through stories is the best way to put you out there. They'll be captivated by you and might even feel inspired. Be your most authentic self. Be as candid as possible. Be honest. Don't fake emotions—be genuine.

Don't lie. People can often tell when you're making something up or trying to impress them.

CHAPTER 2: FIRST IMPRESSIONS

"Almost everyone will make a good first impression,
but only a few will make a good lasting impression."
- Sonya Parker

The first encounter you have with someone has the potential to set the tone of your relationship. Humans are quick to judge and reach conclusions. Therefore, chances are a person starts to develop a perception about you from the moment they see you walk in until the conversation is over. So, how do you make impactful and positive first impressions that cause people to like you and want to hang out with you more?

33

The impression you make within the first few seconds after you meet someone is driven by instinctive reactions. Within seconds, anyone you meet forms an opinion of you. Certain factors influence this impression—how you talk, how you walk, your facial expressions, and how you dress. Do your actions, body language, facial expressions, and gestures align with what you're saying? The combination of these factors largely determines whether the person will like, trust, and respect you. We live in a very visual world. While we often hear the saying, "Don't judge a book by its cover," most people tend to consider the face value of something initially. People want to know who they're interacting with, so they judge every aspect.

In just a glance—less than five seconds—someone you're meeting for the first time forms an idea about you. This is why getting off to a good start is essential. To motivate yourself, you need to consider what's at stake here. Who are you meeting? Why are you meeting them? What significance does this person hold? Once you put the answers to these questions into perspective, you can decide on the body language, word usage, expressions, and clothing that will help set the tone and make things easier for you.

Your appearance, body language, mannerisms, demeanor, and attire will be different when you're going to a job interview than when you're going on a date with your crush.

First impressions have tremendous significance because they can make or break a relationship, and they're nearly impossible to reverse or undo. Hence, knowing how to make a great first impression is essential. There are tons of paid accredited courses being developed today to teach people valuable social skills to make impeccable first impressions. Worry not; I've got your back.

Self-reflect

Before you meet someone new, take some time to think about how you're feeling. Are you confident, relaxed, or nervous? When you take a break and hit pause, you center yourself. This can help you arrange a more positive state of mind. Find a quiet place and do some breathing exercises. Breathe in for seven seconds, hold your breath for two seconds, and then slowly breathe out. Do this at least 13 times. This helps to lower stress. If you're anxious and nervous, change your approach. Tell yourself that meeting this new person will open doors for you. It's an opportunity to usher in happiness. This will bring excitement to your interview, meeting, or date.

<u>Dress Appropriately</u>

Dressing well is an important aspect of a person's presentation. Dressing classy and appropriately is different than being fashionable. Even if fashion isn't your domain, making sure your clothes are clean, crisp, and fit the situation can make a huge difference.

Before leaving for an event, read the invitation and check to see what kind of an occasion it is. Is it a birthday party or a cocktails soirée with a more formal setting? You can't wear shorts to an interview or pants to a day at the beach. Decide your outfit a day before, and set it out. Accessorize it. Show that you put effort into your clothing choice and didn't just throw on the first thing you saw in your closet. Watch, shoes, and fragrance are all important.

Presenting yourself well also includes your physical appearance. Do you need a haircut? Do you need a shave? Check your hygiene. Make sure your teeth are clean. Physical appearance needs to be an utmost priority. The person you're meeting for the first time doesn't know you. They'll initially assess your character based on what you wear and how you look.

The point is not to look like a model who just stepped off a runway but not to appear shabby. Like the axiom says, "A picture is worth a thousand words," so the picture you present needs to illustrate who you are to the person you're meeting. Make sure your appearance and clothing reflect your personality. You often see people who are into gothic clothing and have a bunch of piercings and tattoos. That's their look; it's their way of expressing themselves. Use your fashion and overall look to your advantage. Make sure what you're wearing is appropriate for the situation. It's always better to underdress than to overdress. If you aren't familiar with the country or setting, do research to ensure your clothing is appropriate for the culture and norms.

Be on Time

Our days seem to get shorter and shorter. There's so much to do but so little time. Everyone has commitments and places to be. Time is one of the things in life you can never get back once it's gone. To make the best first impression on someone, start by being on time. In fact, it's better to be early than late. It shows the other person that you value their commitment and making their meeting with you a priority. Someone who's late to important occasions shows a complete disregard for time and a lack of respect for those they're meeting. Especially if you're meeting someone for the first time, they're not going to be interested in hearing your good excuse for running late. Make plans beforehand, and arrive a few minutes early. If you leave early, you give yourself a flexible window in case there are any delays caused by traffic or a wrong turn.

Have a Winning Smile

One smile can make all the difference. If you have a smile on your face, you can make friends anywhere and

38

everywhere—from the grocery store to the meeting room. If you catch someone looking at you, and they appear to be amiable, smile at them. It's amazing how much easier things become if you just learn to smile. Smile while listening to people. Smile when you walk into a room. Always try to smile when shaking hands. Smile when you catch someone staring at you. Practice your smile in front of the mirror. The perfect smile can show some teeth or no teeth at all. Get your smile right. It's a smile that should light up your face and bring a twinkle to your eyes. It should exude positivity and light up the room. A warm and confident smile is welcoming and puts the other person at ease. Smiling is always a winner when it comes to making great first impressions. But don't go overboard. You don't want to come off as insincere or creepy. Keep it genuine.

Be Assertive

First interactions often contain less conversation and more observation. This is when your body language comes into play. Body language can speak louder than words. Use your body language to depict confidence. Walk confidently, and make assured movements.

39

Speak with authority. Form an idea in your head and speak so your confidence comes through. Keep the pitch of your voice low but forceful. Sit or stand with assurance. Stand tall and smile. Make eye contact with whoever you're talking or listening to. Make sure your handshake is firm. Everyone gets a little nervous before meeting someone new. It's natural. To calm the jitters, take a few deep breaths. Lack of confidence can also cause people to exhibit nervous ticks such as nail-biting, sweaty palms, or trembling hands. Recognize your nervous sticks, and look out for them. If you start to experience them, step away from the situation and give yourself a pep talk or do whatever you need to do to calm yourself down.

Be Respectful

When talking to someone, be courteous and attentive. Good manners are essential. Don't engage in cross-talk or whisper to someone nearby. Be polite. Be attentive and courteous. Be on your best behavior. Turn off your mobile. Give the person your full attention. Don't get sidetracked by another conversation. Ask more, and speak less. Stand with your shoulders back. Uncross your arms. Be open and welcoming. Directly face whoever you're talking to. This radiates more positivity.

Be Authentic

Making a good first impression means being you. But you'll also need to fit in to a certain degree. If you're at a business convention, you don't want to start talking about comics or music. Read the room, but, at the same time, you shouldn't lose yourself and pretend to be someone completely different than who you are. Be your authentic self, but tailor your behavior according to the person you're meeting with or the situation.

Be Positive

A positive attitude is a must in a first interaction. Would you prefer to talk to someone who nourishes your energy or someone who dampens it with their negative thoughts? Create a positive impression. You can do this by nurturing positivity in your mind. Before you meet someone, leave all your troubling thoughts and negative energy at home. Think about all the

41

things you like, all the things you enjoy, the people in your life you're grateful for, and the many things you like about yourself. Recall your successes and the compliments you've received in your life. All of these will generate positive energy. When faced with criticism or backlash, remind yourself who you are and all you've accomplished, so others don't affect your energy. Celebrate your successes and practice gratitude. Think of everything you're grateful for—the ability to hear, speak, touch, and see; your good health; adequate clothing; and a roof over your head. This wraps you in warm and positive energy. Be kind to yourself. Don't get down on yourself for minor mistakes. Make use of positive words. Compliment yourself. Don't use words like "can't" or "don't." When you feel positive about yourself, you surround yourself with positivity. If you do this, people will enjoy talking to you.

Match the Energy of the Room

Read the situation and the prevalent emotions, and adapt accordingly. Adjust your behavior, be flexible. Don't change who you are but adjust your energy level and body language to match the mood of your surroundings. If you walk into a formal setting, you don't want to start speaking loudly and cracking jokes. You want to maintain decorum. If someone is talking about their dead pet, be sensitive and sympathize. In the same way, if the vibe is relaxed, don't be too formal.

Focus

Focus your attention on the person you're speaking with. If you're talking to someone, you'd like for them to pay attention because this makes you feel heard, seen, and cared for. Other people are the same. Connect with a person by listening to them. Be present. Don't be distracted. Give them your full attention. Make eye contact, nod. Turn toward them. Don't interrupt or finish their sentences. Don't yawn or look sideways. Don't rush them. Don't look at your phone or your wristwatch to check the time. You might miss what they say or come off as disinterested.

Find Common Ground

Find common topics that you both love talking about,

43

and this will stimulate a refreshing conversation. There's no way they'll be bored or disinterested. You'll have their full attention, and they'll have yours. When the interaction ends, they'll have something to think about and remember you by, and you'll know something about them, which is the beginning of a good connection. Ask questions, and do your research to discover similar interests. Be careful not to ask too many questions, especially personal ones, or it might come off as prying.

CHAPTER 3: BE CONFIDENT

"The most beautiful thing you can wear is
confidence." – Blake Lively

Confidence is necessary in every walk of life, be it social, professional, or personal. You need confidence to try new things, meet new people, overcome personal and professional obstacles, and tackle every challenge. When you're confident in the way you walk and talk, people are attracted to you. There's a certainty and stability in your actions that draws people in. Confidence comes from having great self-esteem. When your self-esteem is soaring, you'll feel confident in your decisions, words, and actions. Confidence and good self-esteem are two essential elements for succeeding in social interactions and becoming popular. Confidence is a state of mind that makes you feel at ease in the most uncomfortable and difficult situations. Your internal source of faith and trust in yourself drives you toward achieving your goals and fulfilling your dreams.

Confidence can help you better articulate your thoughts and get your points across. When you make well-rounded arguments and talk with a purpose, people are more inclined to listen to you. In the same way, if someone walks into a room with hesitant, unsure steps, this telegraphs a lack of confidence. If someone walks in with their head held high, appearing assertive and audacious, their confidence will win over the room. People feel drawn to approach that person and talk with them. Such boldness of presentation takes courage, strength, and sureness of self. This is how you make people want to know you and how you grow into a charismatic version of yourself. So, how do you build this confidence?

Before we begin, remember that every person has limitations, and these can trigger anxiety and nervousness. So, we're not only going to learn how to build confidence but also how to control anxiety. There are many variables—tangible and intangible—that contribute to a successful social interaction, and we can't control all of these. It takes courage to remain strong in the face of the impossible and power through. Confident people are leaders; their confidence in themselves can make others believe in their vision and implement what they say. So, instead of focusing on what we can't control, we engineer our approach to focus on what we can control.

Becoming confident is easier said than done. Trying to appear confident is different than being confident. Our goal is the latter, because it's lasting. However, it requires consistent effort to put yourself out there and let your confidence guide you. Many times, self-doubt will set in and ruin what could have been a perfect engagement. If this happens, don't fret. Go over the exchange in your mind, think about what tripped you up, and figure out a way to do better the next time.

47

Limiting Beliefs

When we're faced with a difficult situation, there are two ways to look at it. Either a person has faith and believes he'll prevail, or he lets self-doubt enter his mind. Self-doubt is an aspect of negative thinking, and it makes a person engage in self-defeating behavior. Self-doubt causes a person to believe they're incapable of accomplishing anything. As a result, their self-esteem plummets. A person with low self-esteem doesn't have the confidence to face people and talk with them. They're always thinking of how other people are better than they are and putting themselves down. This is a self-limiting mindset. Often, when faced with a challenge, our brains get overwhelmed, and we become anxious. It's easier to overthink at this point. Our brain blows everything out of proportion and makes us believe things that aren't true. For example, if you're required to do a task that you've previously done, but you're now required to do it in half the time, a limiting mindset might make you believe you're incapable of completing it. On the flip side, if you had a non-limiting mindset, you'd regard this task as a challenge. If you've done it countless

48

times before, you feel inspired to find a way to decrease the time it takes.

Our inner critic further embellishes a limiting mindset. Everyone has an inner voice. This voice tells us what to do or not do. If we have a negative mindset, this voice becomes our inner critic. Whenever we suffer defeat, this inner critic starts to blame us for everything we did wrong. It makes us believe something is wrong with us, and we might even call ourselves names. In the worst-case scenario, this critic can drive people to engage in self-harm. They become infuriated with themselves, which leads to diminished self-esteem. Such a person believes they'll mess up whatever they do and therefore lacks the confidence to tackle obstacles.

We need to get rid of a limiting mindset and our inner self-critic. A limiting mindset can be countered by having a growth mindset that believes there's no limit to anything, be it your willpower, strength, or abilities. A limiting mindset can be countered by reminding yourself of your previous achievements. Take a paper and pen, and list all of your accomplishments. Call your parents and friends, and ask why they're proud of you. Their belief in you will reaffirm your belief in yourself. All of us were once kids who believed we could do anything, and everything was possible. We only have to regenerate our ability to believe in ourselves again. Make a bet on yourself. Take a chance. Even if you fail, you'll learn from it.

To deal with your inner critic, you need to diminish its negativity. Another thing you can do is make a list of whatever your internal voice is spewing at you. Think objectively about these statements. Is there any truth to them? Are they blown out of proportion or based on facts? Separate facts from opinions. Our brain often converts perceptions and memories into beliefs. When you see something, you already have a preconceived opinion about it. If you have a negative mindset, that will only promote the negative aspect of that perception—like the mistakes you made or the uncomfortable part of the experience. In such a situation, it's better to talk to someone to get a more unbiased perspective on the situation. This will help you move past your negative thoughts and doubts.

Positive Mindset

Negative self-talk, as discussed before, stems from our inner critic, and it damages our self-esteem and outlook on life. To counter this kind of talk, we can make use of positive affirmations. Some examples include: I am strong, I am capable, I am unique, I can do this, I am bigger than my defeats, I have the power to handle this situation, my weaknesses don't define me, my strengths will help me overcome anything. Affirmations reaffirm your faith in yourself. Chant them to yourselves when you wake up every day to start your day on a positive note. Recite them to yourself when you're in the shower. Will yourself to believe in them. Speak them under your breath in uncomfortable situations.

You can also engage in mantra meditation. This requires you to first find a quiet space free of distractions—preferably somewhere in which the sunlight is pouring in. You can do this in your workspace, too. Sit up straight and allow your back to fully support you. Close your eyes, and inhale deeply and slowly for five seconds. Then, slowly exhale.

51

During this time, just focus on your breathing and don't allow any thoughts to interrupt. Keep doing this until you feel no thoughts intruding. When you inhale, imagine positivity and peace entering you and, when you exhale, imagine all negativity leaving your body. Then, repeat affirmations until they feel like reality. At first, it will be hard to center yourself and keep invading thoughts at bay. So start small. Do this practice for five minutes at first and then gradually increase to 10 or 15 minutes. Meditation can help to calm anxiety and nervousness.

A negative mindset is a breeding ground for low self-esteem, low self-worth, and self-doubt. This is why we want to release negative thoughts. There are other creative ways to counter negative thoughts besides positive affirmations, meditation, and confiding in those close to us for support. If you have a bad day, go out for dinner at your favorite restaurant and order your favorite meal. When your mind tries to go back to destructive thoughts, take a bite of your favorite food and be aware of how delicious it is. Or go on a walk in nature. When a negative thought comes to mind, focus on admiring the flowers or the beautiful weather. In this way, you're actively distracting your mind from being negative and ambushing it with positivity. Compose an inner dialogue full of positivity to say to yourself every time negative thoughts come to mind. Recount the good things about the day when destructive thoughts pop up.

Lack of Confidence

To build confidence, you need to identify where it's lacking. Some people might be great speakers but bad at meeting new people. Some people might be good at meeting new people but find it hard to open up. Identifying those weaknesses will help you channel your energy into the right areas. Understand why you lack confidence and where you lack it. Is it because of past trauma caused by harmful incidents when you were a child, criticism from parents, bullying, or harassment? Once you find the reason, work on it.

Remember, you can't hold yourself accountable for the actions of other people. If they were terrible to you, that doesn't mean you have to continue the cycle of beating yourself up. You're a stronger person than you were then. You don't have to let that baggage weigh

53

you down.

Once you've identified an area in which you lack confidence, start working on it. Do you need to be more knowledgeable about a particular topic? Turn to podcasts, videos, books, and mentors to help you gain that knowledge. Do you have trouble speaking up? Start with small steps. Speak up in a friendly environment. Speak up in front of family. Speak up when sitting with colleagues, and then begin to do it among a few unknown people and then groups of people. Take your time to get comfortable in each area.

Do you feel anxiety when doing something for the first time? Access your curiosity. Be curious to know what will happen if you put yourself in this situation that you fear so much. Be curious about what you perceive as your limitations. Put yourself to the test. Either you'll have another accomplishment under your belt or you'll understand where to stop next time. When you're curious, you actively face your fears. When you choose to face your fears, this will give your mind a sense of control over the situation. Since you've purposefully engaged your brain with an activity, it's less likely to focus on the negative.

Do you struggle with not having a sense of humor? Start by going to gig nights or watch videos online. Think of jokes and run them by your friends, focusing on your delivery. Then test them in a larger audience. Collect jokes from other people and mimic them. Create funny anecdotes about experiences in your life.

As you seek to become more confident, think about people who inspire you in this regard. How do they deal with anxiety? What makes them stand out? Is it the command of their voice or their humor? Lastly, don't compare yourself. Comparison leads to the antithesis of confidence. You don't know how many failures the other person has struggled with to get where they are today. Without the whole picture, you're just putting yourself down, which puts you three steps back. We want to gain confidence, not lose it.

You can also work with a therapist to deal with issues that affect your confidence. These licensed professionals have the experience to assist you in growing. If your negative patterns are too entrenched, you might be asked to engage in behavioral therapy, which takes one aspect of your behavior at a time, explores it, and applies effective remedies. For example, people with a poor self-image sometimes are encouraged to exercise more. This is because exercise helps release endorphins, which are feel-good hormones that reside in the brain. When you feel good overall, you'll naturally feel better about yourself.

CHAPTER 4: BE MAGNETIC

"Charisma is a sparkle in people that money can't buy. It's an invisible energy with visible effects."
- Marianne Williamson

People who are liked by everyone are rare. These people have magnetic charisma. Their aura pulls in anyone they talk to or walk by. They influence others without even trying to. These people are popular and adored by everyone around them. Being magnetic is a powerful characteristic that must be cultivated if you want people to like you and listen to what you have to say. So, how do you achieve that?

To become someone magnetic, you have to get noticed. People who have a fascinating vibe don't take long to get noticed. People go out of their way to introduce themselves to such individuals. No matter what they say, they command attention. They're confident regardless of what situation they're in.

Charisma is a hard thing to define. It's often considered to be a quality handed down from the heavens. The word "charisma" comes from the Greek words for favor and grace. It's defined as a special quality, a magical quality, that's magnetic and invokes loyalty and enthusiasm. It makes someone more appealing. Having charisma is much more than being a good talker, good-looking, or likable. It means having an inviting personality that allows you to connect with people from all walks of life. You're able to engage with anyone regardless of your relationship to them. A charismatic person makes a good impression on whoever they meet, and people are more inclined to listen to them and do as they say.

People with a magnetic personality don't develop this

overnight but spend years bettering their social and emotional skills to make sure they can engage with people authentically.

Each of us has a certain level of inherent charisma. We all know someone who looks up to and is inspired by us. Here's an exercise: Have that person write down why they like you and what about you inspires them. If someone views you in a positive light, you may have some qualities you can amplify to become more appealing and magnetic.

Most people believe charisma is the ability to attract and enthrall others. This is why people go out of their way to make others like them. They buy presents, pay compliments, do whatever they're asked, and more. However, sometimes this has the reverse effect in your attempts to make people respect you. If you genuinely want other people to like you, you have to make them feel important in a way that doesn't decrease your importance. A charismatic person isn't arrogant when he talks to someone, but, rather, he makes them feel worthy. He gives them the sense that he values their opinions and heeds what they say without going overboard. When others feel valued, this creates loyalty.

To move from being forgettable to fascinating is a feat many have embarked on, but only some have achieved. Luckily for you, the techniques discussed below will help you become the magnetic icon you strive to be.

Below are four attributes that will help you improve your interpersonal skills, likeability, and magnetism.

Body Language

Body language includes everything from expressions on your face to what you do with your hands. Practice using shorthand gestures that are firm and assertive. Charm the other person with inviting eyes. Your eyes transmit the life and light inside you. If the expression in them is bubbly, playful, and joyful, the other person will be inclined to return those expressions. You don't just smile with your mouth; you smile with your eyes, too, when the corners crinkle or there's a glint of light. This exudes confident energy and makes you appear more welcoming. While talking to other people, always

60

maintain eye contact, but don't stare. This creates a memorable impression.

People who smile and laugh seem more trustworthy. See how others react to you by observing their body language and adjust your tactics accordingly. Mimic their body language, and don't overdo your gestures. Keep them minimal. Small gestures are the best, and they're necessary. They break the monotony in a conversation. Respect other people's space. Don't touch them without asking. Stand an arm's length away. Be mindful of how much you blink. Blinking too much indicates you're uncomfortable, but, as mentioned before, don't stare, as this can make others feel uncomfortable.

Master your handshake. If your handshake is firm and strong, this makes the best first impression. Gently take the other person's hand and then apply pressure. Don't pump your hand up and down too much. Let the other person release your hand first, or it may appear you're in a rush.

Like we talked about before, the postures of both

people engaged in the conversation are important. Your posture indicates how confident you are. Walk with your back straight, and don't be too firm or too casual in your stride. Maintain control of your body, your hand gestures, and your facial expressions. As long these are under control, it doesn't matter so much whether your words are precise. Sit up straight. Reciprocate the energy you get from the other person. If the other person brings everything to the conversation, make sure you do the same. Match their energy.

Your body posture must convey openness, as this is more inviting. Don't have your arms or legs crossed or your face averted. Have your body facing forward in an open posture, not guarded by crossed arms or legs. Don't slouch or hunch up your shoulders. Don't make fists with your hands. Keep your neck straight and your head erect. Lean in when talking to people. Listen with your whole body. Don't just try to help. Really listen. Empathize with what's being said. Keep listening until the other person is done talking. If you have to cut the other person off to clarify something, apologize, and don't do it too often. Ask follow-up questions.

Paraphrase and repeat what you heard to show the other person you were really listening.

Create Memorable Conversations

In any conversation, be forthright about what you feel. Be honest and open. Be genuine about your feelings, so you're easy to trust. Don't fake anything. Think on your feet. Be humorous. Always have some anecdotes and funny stories at the ready to keep the conversation entertaining. Study your favorite comedians to learn how they turn simple, daily events into humor. The way you deliver the joke has a lot to do with how funny it seems to your listeners. You can develop your wit and sense of humor by learning to accept whatever's being said and then adding to it. Don't defend or deflect. Have a quick wit.

Emphasize your potential rather than your achievements; otherwise, you'll come off as tooting your own horn. Get people to talk about themselves. Being a good listener means giving other people importance and making them feel you're interested in them. It also helps you understand the other person's mindset. People enjoy talking about themselves. This makes them feel good and, therefore, they'll associate you with positive feelings. It helps if you share with them as well. When you share things that are important to you, people feel valued and trusted. This helps to create a stronger bond.

Seek common ground when talking with another person so you both can share enthusiastically. This is a great way to draw someone out of their shell and make them feel at ease. Use open-ended questions when starting up a conversation, and then subtly chime in. When you find the smallest indicator of common ground, use it as a building block to create rapport. Use language such as, "I agree, I can relate," to establish a connection.

One of the most effective ways to engage your audience is through storytelling. Storytelling can be described as the art of communication using stories and narratives. Stories make us experience information, as opposed to just consuming it. It gives an emotional background to what you're trying to say. Storytelling enables the listener to convert the ideas presented in the story into their own ideas and experiences. This makes the content more personal and relatable. Storytelling also creates a mirroring pattern in the brain, allowing the listeners to experience similar brain activity as the storyteller. This allows greater understanding and builds motivation amongst the listeners.

Enthusiasm

We're drawn to people who give us energy—people who are upbeat, enthusiastic, and optimistic—and we feed off the energy of a confident person. To achieve this dynamic connection with others, think of entertaining and inspiring them, no matter what's happening around you. Resist the temptation to complain or volley insults. Instead, find positive, arousing, or humorous topics to discuss.

Confidence is one of the most attractive human qualities. It speaks more about you than can be said in your résumé. Confident people are universally appealing. They are easy to work with, trustworthy, and inspiring for others. Their inviting attitude attracts people around them. Showing confidence

65

through your body language, eye contact, smile, and handshake makes people around you feel secure.

Become a More Interesting Person

How you feel about yourself is translated into your actions. Surround yourself with positivity and celebrate your achievements. Work toward success so you're always accomplishing something and have a positive mindset, which breeds charisma. Magnetism and confidence can be enhanced by becoming a more interesting person. Find a way to lead a more interesting life. Make a list of ten things you've never done but always wanted to do, and then do them! Always have three great stories to tell. Be enthusiastic and motivating. Become comfortable in your skin. Respect yourself. Appreciate yourself for who you are instead of picking yourself apart. Fall in love with yourself. Live from and by your values.

CHAPTER 5: SHOW INTEREST

"The deepest principle in human nature is the craving to be appreciated." – William James

As we talked about before, being a charismatic person and a person who can influence the opinions of others has a lot to do with making other people feel important, which causes them to be drawn to you. When you show interest in other people, they're naturally drawn toward you.

Pay Attention

Face the person you're talking to, and remove all distractions. If you're texting while talking, you aren't giving the other person your complete attention. This makes them feel less worthy of your time. Pay attention to every word so your reaction to their stories is genuine, and your facial cues reflect that. You raise your eyebrows, your eyes open wider, or the sides of your mouth will drop to reveal your true reaction. When you face someone, you allow them to see your responses. This tells them you're generally interested in hearing them speak.

Take time to reflect on what the other person has said to respond appropriately. Start speaking only after the person has finished. Speak with intention, whether that be to help, to support, to provide a solution, or to reciprocate.

Listen with intention. This helps to ensure that you're focused and not losing interest. Why are you getting to know this person? Why do you want to know this specific story? What result do you hope to achieve?

68

Listen with a purpose at the back of your mind.

One of the most difficult obstacles to overcome is to stop thinking about the things that bother you and stay present in the moment. If you have trouble staying away from anxious thoughts, remember the fact that thinking about these things won't solve your problems. When an anxious thought appears, remember that there's nothing you can do about it at that moment, and there's no reason why you should allow it to ruin an opportunity to make new acquaintances. Also, avoid focusing too much on your posture, tone, and the way you speak. This will make you even more self-conscious and break the subtle yet pleasant course of the conversation.

Be Genuinely Intrigued

If you want people to be interested in you, you must first be interested in them. Empathize with them. Offer them help. Dissect parts of the story to better your understanding and show them you genuinely care. Then, once they've told you their story, you can share your troubles or experiences. Mutual sharing helps build a deeper level of connection.

Ask open-ended questions. This gives the other person the opportunity to elaborate. For example, don't just ask questions that have a yes or no answer, such as, "Do you like your boss?" Instead, rephrase the question to open up the conversation: "Yikes, I heard that's a tough workplace. What's it like?" This shows you're engaged and curious, which leads to a deeper conversation.

Don't let the conversation die after the other person finished talking. Instead, you can keep the course of the conversation going by stating your commentary or mention something similar that happened to you. Then follow up with another logical or interesting question. Participating in the conversation with your observations and experiences will prevent the other person from feeling like they're being interrogated.

Be Sincere

If you let the other person manage the conversation, you'll often find it utterly boring. Take an active part in the discussion by asking questions, really listening, and paying attention, and then contribute your opinions and tidbits. In the process, you can change the topic to something you find more interesting. Offer stories of your own. React to the other person's stories the way you want them to react to your yours. Don't do or say something for the sake of saying it. Only do/say it if you genuinely believe in it. Don't change the way you act when you're in the presence of a particular person. Act the same way as you would normally. Use your body language to convey how sincere you are. Maintain steady eye contact but don't stare. Your eye contact shows you're paying attention; if your gaze goes in all directions, it indicates you're losing interest. People will notice and become turned off. Don't be too intense, as it might come off as cocky or that you're trying to be intimidating. At the same time, don't be too relaxed, as you'll appear uninterested.

When someone is speaking, keep an open mind. Accept everything that's being said without judgment. The world we live in is becoming more diverse and evolving by the minute; something we know to be true today might not be true tomorrow. So, we have to be sensitive to and mindful of that. We have to respect the truth and originality of the other person. Develop a genuine curiosity to learn more about the thoughts and feelings of others.

Pay attention to whether the things you say make people feel more comfortable and at ease, or they introduce tension. When you focus on saying encouraging things and displaying compassion, you can help a person feel comfortable around you even when the situation itself isn't comfortable.

Respect the Opinions of Others

You should always avoid telling a person they're wrong, especially when meeting them for the first time. People have their own stories and experiences from which they form their opinions. You can ask them to elaborate about why they think or feel the way they do, or you can simply accept it.

Be open to new perspectives. Try to understand the long view of others. If you refuse to consider why another person thinks or feels the way they do, you can't develop a sincere interest in and a strong relationship with them. If you try to understand their point of view, you aren't abandoning your own. You're just learning another perspective. Hearing their opinion will help you learn about the other person's life experiences and allow you to view life through a different lens. This only amplifies your knowledge of the world and will help you connect with more people in the future. For example, if someone has a different musical taste than you do, don't criticize it. Try to understand what they find appealing about it. Maybe it's the lyrics or the singer or the loud bass that makes them want to dance, or perhaps the music is associated with a memory from a happy time.

Politics and religion are often topics of conflict, which is why people steer clear of them. If you have to discuss them, try to understand the other person's values before judging. Listen with the purpose of asking sincere questions, and do your best not to argue.

Make Them Feel Appreciated

Everyone wants to feel special, so a strong starting

73

point is to make them feel great about themselves. If they've had a "win" of some kind, mention that, congratulate them, and show them they're special in your mind. People love being credited or rewarded for something. Whenever you discover something unique about a person, pay them a compliment. Be generous, but don't overdo it. Also, be specific with your compliments. A vague comment like, "Hey, I love your look" could be made more precise and impactful: "Wow, the color of your shirt compliments your eyes." It's specific and therefore more genuine.

If you hint at something or make a suggestion that the other person then expresses more fully, allow them the pleasure of thinking it was their idea. If we're truly only seeking to build a long-term relationship, why should we care about who gets the credit? Why not let someone else have the spotlight as long as we achieve what we're out to get?

Make Them Feel Important

Make others feel important. When you first talk to someone, your main goal should be encouraging them

74

to talk about themselves. Ask them random questions. Ask them about their favorite holiday and why it's their favorite. Once you get them to start sharing, they'll feel encouraged to talk more deeply about themselves because they're talking about things they're interested in.

Chapter 6: Listen with Intention

"We have two ears and one mouth so that we can listen twice as much as we speak."

— Epictetus

The best strategy for developing your listening skills is to understand how to listen. The art of listening is seldom talked about, but it holds massive importance. Many people believe they know how to listen to someone and pay attention, but the reality is quite different. Most people start to zone out, get distracted, lose focus, interrupt or talk over the other person, or don't give them enough space and time to be vulnerable. Paying attention is the absolute key to having a great conversation. It's an essential social skill and will help you better your relationships and cultivate deeper connections. We're now going to talk about the proper technique for listening.

Listen Actively

When you talk with someone, you need to focus on what they're saying. Accept who they are, what they're saying, and their opinions without any judgment. Acknowledge what they're telling you by using words like "Absolutely," "Obviously," or "I agree." This is vital to create rapport with the person you're talking with. People will feel you genuinely care about what they have to say and will truly appreciate your company. Most of us are terrible listeners because we aren't present in the moment—not just present physically but mentally, too. Your mind shouldn't wander, and you should be focused on what the other person is saying. It's tough to keep your mind tethered to one place for a long time, but if your mind starts to wander frequently and for long periods, the other person will

78

notice.

If your mind wanders during conversations, try focusing on breathing into your belly for one full breath every time your mind wanders. This will bring you back to the moment and allow you to focus on the person talking again.

After a person is done speaking, the best course of action is to summarize what they told you. This shows them you're trying to grasp the situation. Also, if you missed something, they'll fill you in. This will help you respond well and provide more rational and organized feedback.

While the other person is talking, it's best not to interrupt them. If you have a comment or a question, wait until the other person is done speaking to say it. Chiming in on a conversation shouldn't be done at the expense of cutting someone off mid-sentence. When you interrupt someone, you sideline that person. They feel their voice or story isn't worthy of being heard, and they may resent you instead of being mesmerized by you. So, when the other person stops speaking, wait two seconds and then speak up. Or first ask them if they want to add something before you give your response. These two seconds might feel too long when you first start practicing this, but eventually, that pause becomes an instinct. Ask follow-up questions of the other person. Truly get to the bottom of what they're trying to tell you before offering any advice or help. This encourages the other person to continue speaking.

Remember Names

A person's name is their identity. It's something they hold close to themselves. It's a part of who they are. Legendary success writer Dale Carnegie once said that a person's name is the sweetest and most important sound in any language. You can understand people's affinity for their name because people often get it tattooed on their bodies or wear a necklace that displays it. The point is, names are important to people, so, if you want to build a conversation with someone, use their name repeatedly. This technique is used by those who are charismatic and magnetic. Remembering someone's name and using it in

80

conversation will get you far and makes a great impression. Saying their name creates an immediate rapport with them.

It's the worst feeling when you're at a social gathering chatting away and someone walks up to you—someone who's probably extremely important—and you can't recall their name. It's even more awful if they remember your name. They might be expecting you to address them by name as well or introduce them to the person you were talking to, and that's really awkward. Therefore, it's important to remember someone's name so you can address them during a conversation. If you forget their name, don't panic. Don't start sweating or losing your cool. Don't stammer or overthink. Gain control of the situation by greeting the person warmly and engaging with them confidently. If the conversation shifts from small talk to a lengthy discussion, it then becomes necessary for you to know their name. At this point, admit your flaw and ask them their name, but do this with confidence. If you're weak and awkward about it, the whole atmosphere will change to one of disappointment. But, if you deal with the situation with confidence and a positive approach, you can avoid all that. Admit your fault and say, "Hey, I have a bad memory for names. Could you please remind me of your good name, Mr.____," and let them fill in the name for you. As soon as they do, acknowledge it by saying, "Yes, right, thank you. I'm making a mental note now. This is embarrassing for me, but it won't happen again." Then make a real effort to remember their name.

No matter how hard we try, we still forget someone's name now and then. And that's okay. We meet many people every day, so it's hard to keep track of everyone's name amid the hustle and bustle. The best course of action is always to apologize, politely say, "I'm terribly sorry, but I've forgotten your name. Could you please tell it to me again?" It's that simple. Of course, doing this repeatedly isn't good, but doing it once or twice—especially when you're caught in a bind—is all right. Ask them as soon as you realize you've forgotten their name. The longer you wait to ask their name and the longer you keep talking, the more offended they'll be when they realize you'd forgotten their name all this while. So, ask at the start, before any words are said.

Having to ask for someone's name makes us feel guilty. It indicates to the other person that they weren't important enough for you to remember their name, which we never want to happen. If your memory fails you, here are some other techniques to help you deal with these difficult situations as smoothly as possible.

When You're Making Introductions

When you want to introduce yourself to someone you've already met before, simply walk up to them, stick out your hand, and say your name: "Hi, I'm Jack. We met at the business convention." Chances are, they'll respond in the same way by introducing themselves by name. Many times, other people will forget your name, too. So this gets you both off the hook! By taking the initiative, you make the situation easier for both of you.

Don't play the guessing game if you see someone you've met before but can't immediately recall their name. If you start guessing their name and call them by an incorrect name, the other person might take offense. This will ultimately jeopardize the connection you two might have started to build the last time you met. No doubt, having someone call you by a name other than your own feels worse and more offensive than simply asking them for their name again. So, if you can't remember someone's name, just simply say, "Excuse me, what's your name again?" The person is likely to respond with just their first name. Now, here's a sly little trick. If they do this, respond with a charming laugh, smile, and say, "Of course, but I want to know your last name." You save yourself with a curveball. Knowing their last name will help you remember their full name better the next time. People are more forgiving when we forget their last name than their first name. With this technique, you get both names, and they don't discover you'd forgotten their name.

However, this technique can backfire if they respond by asking, "My first or last name?" In that case, be earnest and say you want to know their first name. On one occasion, I panicked and said, "Last name," because I didn't want them to find out I'd forgotten their first name, and we were well into the conversation. Luckily for me, they said, "Beckett, Carl

Beckett." Their James Bond-like reply saved me. On another occasion, someone responded with, "McGuire," but I thought quickly and referred to them as "Mr. McGuire" in my next sentence.

When You're Parting Ways

When the two of you are saying your goodbyes, and you realize you can't remember the other person's name, ask if they have a business card to take home with you. If you forget their name later, you can take out their card. Not only will this help you refresh your memory, but it will also show them that it was important to you to have their business card.

Be Present

When someone is speaking, you must pay attention and be present. Try to etch their name into your brain. We're all inattentive listeners at times. We all become victims of conversational narcissism and start waiting for the moment to jump in and contribute our two cents to the topic. So, if you're focusing on what you're going to say when someone tells you their name, it will go in one ear and out the other. Make sure you're paying attention when they say their name. Be as attentive as possible during introductions.

Repeat Their Name Often

When the other person says their name, repeat it after them. You can say something along the lines of, "It's a pleasure to meet you, Jacob," or, "Bree, what a nice name." You might ask them what their name means or to spell it, especially if it's an unusual name. If it's a common name that has different spelling variations, ask them the variation they use. Compliment their name. Ask them who chose it for them or the story behind it. This will make their name stand out more in your mind and make them more memorable after that meeting. Also, using their name throughout the conversation will help to build muscle memory. A good practice is always to say it one last time when saying goodbye. It's charming and helps you remember the name.

Be Empathetic

Empathy is the key to nurturing a relationship. We need to respect other people's stories, their personal space, and them as a person. Being a good listener doesn't mean that you just become a wall for the whole conversation. It means lending an ear and then offering empathy. Say a few words now and then to let the speaker know you're still present. Make use of statements indicating your concern during the conversation, such as, "You're right," or, "That's amazing," or, "That's so nice of you." Let your eye contact, gestures, facial expressions, and hand movements express empathy, and use them often during the conversation. Making eye contact shows the other person you're sincere and that they have your undivided attention.

Try to convey emotions with your facial expressions. Opening your mouth slightly and raising your eyebrows indicates surprise. Frown when you hear something sad, or nod with a consoling smile.

Gently rubbing someone's back or holding their hand also conveys empathy, but this may not be appropriate in all situations. Try to feel the emotion emanating from the conversation, and react to it genuinely. Try to imagine how it must have felt for that person when they experienced what they're describing. That emotion will naturally appear in your facial expression, and the speaker will notice it. This forms a deeper connection.

Your body language can help convey empathy in a lot of ways. Tilt your head slightly as you listen to the other person talk. This shows them you're interested in what they have to say. Nod during the conversation to show you're paying attention, and keep an open posture. Be relaxed, sit upright, and let your arms rest naturally. Your legs can be loosely apart, but don't cross your arms or legs. Lean in slightly when you speak. Do this when you're seated; leaning in while standing looks awkward. Lean in when someone is sharing the most critical part of their story. If the other person is telling a joke, do it near the punch line.

Good listening skills are a significant part of effective communication. People with refined communication skills can maneuver through any social situation. If you genuinely listen to what people are saying, you make them feel appreciated and understood. People are drawn to those who show they care for and value them.

88

If you want to be charismatic, you need to become a good listener. As Dale Carnegie also said, "You can make more friends in two months by becoming interested in other people than you can in two years by trying to get other people interested in you."

It's a fantastic feeling to have someone entirely focused on you. You feel as if you're in the spotlight just by being in their presence. Take in every word the other person says and value what they're saying. Never judge, insult, or belittle. Speak sparingly, but be present.

CHAPTER 7: THE ART OF PERSUASION AND INFLUENCE

"People almost invariably arrive at their beliefs not on the basis of proof but on the basis of what they find attractive." – Blaise Pascal

There are many occasions when we want to influence another person. You might want your employer to give you a raise or promotion or have the cashier at the supermarket provide you with a discount or create a business partnership with someone. We can get many things in life by simply tapping into our power of persuasion. You can sometimes accomplish this by using reason, or you can develop qualities in your personality that allow you to sway others without having to reason with them.

The most powerful form of persuasion and influence isn't in the words you say; it's in who you are. Masterful persuasion comes from a person first being influenced by who you are rather than what you say. Let's look into some tactics that allow you to influence anyone.

Project Confidence

The first order of business is to remain confident and project confidence. Always imagine yourself at the top of the world. Feel as if you're mighty. Give yourself compliments and root for yourself. Let confidence flow through your body. Let it affect your stance, your walk, and how you dress. The more confident you are, the more convincing your argument will sound, and, hence, the more powerful you'll appear. You'll have faith in what you're saying, so you won't fumble or stutter; you'll put forth solid points with conviction. When people see someone so sure of themselves, they feel compelled to listen to them.

Always act with confidence, so it becomes a part of who you are. A study conducted by the University of Leicester found that the single significant behavioral difference between persuaders and persuadees was the degree of confidence expressed.

Confidence shows the other person that you're dedicated and you have self-assurance.

People Are More Likely to be Persuaded by Someone They Like

Make use of flattery and kind words. If a person likes you and gets good vibes from you, they can easily be influenced by you. Don't be too obvious with the flattery, and don't go overboard, because people will catch on. For example, instead of telling your superior, "Hey, boss, I love your shoes. Can I take tomorrow off?" say, "Hey, can I please take tomorrow off? I know you're flexible and always accommodating, but I still wanted to run this by you to make sure there won't be an issue."

93

The first statement is too blunt and sounds exactly like what it is—flattery. The second statement subtly compliments the other person but also gets the job done.

Make It Seem Beneficial for the Other Party

You can influence anyone if you make it seem they'll win. Make your request seem valuable to the other party. This can be tricky, but with some wordplay and proper reasoning, you can do it. For example, if you're trying to convince a colleague or a classmate that you barely know to help you with something, first find out if they need help with something. Then, introduce yourself. Be warm and cheerful. Ask them if they need help, and let them know you're happy to help them out. Then, wait for some time to pass, and make your request to them.

If they don't need help with anything, make food part of the agreement, discuss how fun the process will be, or tell them what a learning opportunity it will be for them, etc. Make use of logic and use intelligent words.

94

Words should exhibit positivity, motivation, and enthusiasm.

Let Your Reputation Speak for You

If I want to make a name for myself in a new circle, I need to ensure that my affiliations with other circles are strong so I have some skills under my belt, and the people in my new circle already know my reputation. This is how celebrities are able to influence anyone with their charisma. Everyone knows who they are and how they act, so they don't need to do much or say much to influence anyone to do something for them. It happens naturally. Start to build your portfolio in a similar way.

Be Patient but Persistent

This is perhaps the most crucial message. When you're trying to influence anyone, you're essentially seeking to align their beliefs with yours. This will only happen if they like you or see how agreeing with you will benefit them or if you successfully persuade them. If you're unsuccessful in influencing an individual, don't

95

become desperate and start pleading, begging, or arguing. Instead, let it go, collect yourself, and think about what could have gone wrong and what you'd like to do differently the next time. Approach them again at a later time. Your persuasion skills—and whatever influence you achieved that first time around—might have made an impression, so when you make the next effort, your chances of success are stronger. Don't abandon your goal. Be patient on this journey, and don't give up. The power of persuasion is a skill that requires time to be honed and finessed. You won't be successful all the time, but you'll become more skilled and natural at it with practice and proper tactics.

How to Motivate Others to Do What You Want Them to Do

Throughout the previous chapters of this book, we defined and emphasized the importance of possessing and exuding charisma to advance in all areas of life. As you learned, charisma is a trait nurtured through devotion to yourself and your core value system. It manifests in your awareness of what you stand for and expressing it with your body language, facial

96

expressions, speech, actions, and appearance. For someone who is yet to start your journey, this is easier said than done. Of course, if living and acting on your best intentions were so easy, everyone would be doing it.

Without a doubt, journeying through life will require overcoming obstacles. Some of them are more obvious (e.g., gaining skills and competencies, getting to know people, and building your reputation). However, being at the very top of the ladder (a spot reserved for those who not only play roles in society but also build and grow companies and organizations and work to make a difference in the world) takes overcoming one more obstacle: learning how to influence others.

You see, your heart may be in the right place, and what you stand up for may make complete sense in your mind (and perhaps even in the minds of others). However, when you're working on spreading new messages and sharing original ideas, one of your tasks will be to persuade others to join in. There's a chance that individuals and groups who play an important role in the fulfillment of your mission may not see things the way you do, so you'll have to give them a nudge. Say you want to start a charity. You'll have to persuade people that your plan has a true impact on society. Or, if you're applying for a business loan, you'll have to convince the decision-makers that your business plan truly has a chance of success. For this, you'll need to develop the skill to influence.

Now, if your heart is in the right place (as it is the case with most people), there's a chance that you think that influencing is the same as manipulation. But what if it's not? If you think about it, "manipulating" means to give a false presentation of yourself and to use other people for personal gain. Manipulation is harmful to those who are being used, while influence isn't.

The key difference between manipulation and influence is that being influential doesn't abuse people's weaknesses and insecurities. Instead, it means wielding the power that comes from your integrity and confidence to convey a message people will believe. But it won't be because they're being lied to but because they trust your judgment and put their faith in your abilities. Much like the people you're aiming to influence, you too are being influenced every day. Either consciously or subconsciously, your decisions and actions are based on the trust in judgment and opinions of those you find trustworthy— whether it's your spouse, family, doctor, teacher, or a politician. So why wouldn't you be one of those people, and more importantly, how do you become one?

Being a charismatic leader means becoming a figure of influence. A charismatic leader, as research found, is someone who has a strong presence. On the other hand, being pleasant in appearance and approachable is a part of affability, which is the second key characteristic of charismatic leaders. As it turns out, people are very good at evaluating their level of charisma. Research also shows that if you were to rate how charismatic you are on a scale of 1–5, you would probably be right.

Before we delve further into this chapter, I'd like you to pause for a second and rate your level of charisma. Now, it's time to compare where you are now with the level you want to be at. If you don't think of yourself as being as charismatic as you'd like, there's also a good chance you know the reasons for that. What are the leadership traits and qualities you want to work on? If you're unsure which of the key skills and competencies need additional boosting, this chapter will present you with some traits and skills you can work on.

The key influences to develop if you want to become a charismatic leader are presence, leadership skills, and affability. This list may be short, but it encompasses a wide range of personal strengths, skills, and competencies to develop first.

Presence

Having a strong presence is the number-one trait of charismatic leaders. However, this trait encompasses four different characteristics to develop: confidence, self-esteem, optimism, and resilience. You see, as a leader, you will get all the perks of being influential. You'll get the spotlight and the power to make decisions, which will manifest in money, assets, and quality personal relationships. But with great powers come great responsibilities. You'll need to have the courage to step out first and fight for your goal, make plans, decide the right course of action, and accept the responsibility for risks and failures. This will take knowing how to predict and overcome obstacles and knowing how to solve problems.

Now perhaps it's a bit clearer why only a handful of people dare to lead. First, it takes a considerable amount of confidence to carry out this role. You need other people to believe that you can do the things you set out to do, and you need to believe that you're able to do them. Many people are good at convincing others, but not so much themselves. This is why indecisiveness, risky actions, and ineffective ones take place.

Your effectiveness and power as a charismatic leader grow with confidence and faith in your abilities. Your confidence, on the other hand, will grow with the ability to communicate across a variety of settings, groups, and individuals. Public speaking is perhaps the biggest challenge for one's confidence, and practicing it surely benefits your growth.

Aside from being confident, charismatic people are also optimistic. It shouldn't be difficult to understand why people want to follow those who built them up and not those who beat them down. So ask yourself which effect you think your presence has on the people around you. People are very good at detecting superficial, false optimism. Your task will be to nurture a genuinely positive outlook on everyday situations, even the challenging ones.

Being genuinely positive means making an effort to see the best in different situations, events, and people. However, to act in this way in all cases takes developing a good emotional compass and knowing what kind of positive outlook is appropriate for the moment. Let's say you're attending a meeting during which you found out that the organization needs to fire a certain amount of people. What's the right measure of optimism to use here? Surely, this is not the time to be overly cheerful. Instead, you can frame the situation as temporarily ending working relationships for the sake of long-term stability.

If you were the one to fire those people, what would be an appropriate thing to tell them? Remember, many of these people need consolation and encouragement.

Many of these people would lose their jobs with loans and mortgages to pay or sick family members to support. If you were to practice charismatic leadership in this situation, what would you do? Undoubtedly, assuring those being let go that their skills, talents, and contribution will always be appreciated is the first step. It also helps to share a couple of supportive sentences about the direction they could take to grow their career going forward.

These would be genuine expressions of optimism in potentially defeating situations. How you leave things with people around you undoubtedly sets the tone for how you'll be seen in the eyes of those who you depend on. The fruits of being empathetic won't fail to show.

In the long run, positive communication helps you establish yourself as someone trustworthy and capable of managing problems, all while taking care of those who depend on you. This allows people around you to feel more optimistic, and you want that, whether they're above or below your rank. This is because those who are below you can push you up, and those who are above you can give a helping hand so that you reach the next level.

Both positive thinking and a positive outlook on events taking place, as you can see, create powerful tools in solving problems and negotiating solutions, whether it's at work or home.

While you can use your influence for both positive and negative purposes, keep in mind that the former yields lasting betterment for yourself and others in the long run, while the latter only has temporary benefits. The most powerful type of influence is the one that unites people around a common cause, and personal progress and benefits become only the side effects of it.

Leadership Skills

People with strong leadership skills grow and nurture them actively and on purpose, although it may seem that their charisma is God-given. Leadership is a matter of intent, decision, and action—first on self-improvement and then on fulfilling your mission and goals. Successful leaders use different leadership styles, all developed with hard work. These competencies help them convey their vision and messages in different settings and to different people, tailored around the circumstances and individual traits of those they lead. This is done using strong communication skills.

Affability

Developing the skill of conveying an attractive, inviting presence that inspires people to talk to you, engage in your plans, and listen to what you have to say is the third most important leadership quality. If you think of any leader you respect (be it Tony Robbins, Oprah Winfrey, or even Aragorn from the *Lord of the Rings*), what do you see these people having in common? They make you feel good about yourself, and they make you feel even better about yourself when you imagine being in their presence. You want to talk to them, confide in them, share your biggest fears and insecurities, and ask for their guidance on what to do to solve your problems. All of these individuals are affable. They all make people feel good and comfortable. But how do you develop this ability?

The best way to become affable is to work on growing your emotional intelligence. Tuning your emotional radar will help you understand people's feelings, motives, and actions better. It teaches you how to speak to them and share your message.

Another important part of being affable is being optimistic, which we thoroughly discussed in the previous section. But to have an optimistic outlook also requires knowing how to command your feelings so that your behavior doesn't come across as exaggerated or superficial. It will help you appeal to the best in other people so that you can direct the relationship toward what you want to achieve.

Aside from this, charismatic people are good at knowing when to show and when to hide their feelings. Of course, acting the way you feel isn't suitable or effective in all situations. In many of them, it can be quite harmful. Powerful leaders maintain a unique serene exterior, with the hustle and the work needed in growing their vision hidden from sight. This isn't lying, as it may appear. Acting in this way allows other people to focus on the essence of what you're trying to say. It helps to emphasize your key message.

Say you want to inspire people to follow your training program. Do they need to know you're struggling financially because of your student loan? Not really. Nowhere in your job description does it say they do or that it affects your credibility. So why would they have known about how you hustled to secure the funds for starting your business? Rest assured, they only want to see your rock-solid muscles and hear all about how to grow them with your assistance.

Being interesting to other people is another common trait of approachable leaders. A polished look and a smile on your face make you charming. The same is true when you have listening, communication, and storytelling skills and use appropriate optimism and humor.

How to Become More Appealing

People want to be around interesting people. Aside from the traits already mentioned (i.e., confidence, optimism, listening skills, and communication skills), here are a couple more skills to develop to become attractive to other people:

1. *Passion and drive:* Being passionate about the things you love and the job you do is inspiring. It draws people to you, as it appeals to their inner drive and passions. Being passionate gives meaning to mundane, everyday tasks, and being the one to remind people of that makes you a person they look up to.

2. *Courage:* Leadership means handling gigantic responsibilities, evaluating and making business deals, making bold decisions, and taking risks for the sake of everyone's personal growth and the fulfillment of the common goal. Learning how to be bold and brave means nurturing confidence and resilience to frustration, stress, fear, and failure.

3. *Humor:* The ability to make people laugh conveys confidence, but it also helps other people stay optimistic in the face of challenges. Learning how to use appropriate humor by analyzing the work of other leaders you admire, as well as your favorite comedians, will help establish yourself as a person people can turn to when they feel discouraged and need a confidence boost.

Now that you know why it is important to be charismatic, let's start practicing it, shall we?

As mentioned earlier, there are good chances that you can accurately evaluate how charismatic you are. If you're not completely happy with your result, you can start practicing some of the techniques to nurture personal charisma. The fact is that you can significantly grow your personal magnetism in a matter of weeks if you only practice daily and consistently. There are particular steps you can take to notice an improvement in less than a month!

Without further ado, here are the strategies to become more charismatic:

1. *Let your inner self shine through your outfit.* Whether it's business attire, casual chic, or romantic flare, your style can do a great service to help you communicate your inner self. Before anything else, people around you will notice your outfit. The best part is that you can dress into suitable, stylish, and original outfits on any budget. However, the main rule is to only wear those items that spark joy. Whichever piece of clothing you put on, make sure it makes you feel happy and comfortable. Discomfort hurts charisma because people can spot that you feel uncomfortable.

2. *Practice eye contact.* Finding a good measure of pleasant, genuine, and appropriate eye contact will take exercise. To learn how to make impactful eye contact, hold it only a second longer than usual. The ultimate achievement is to maintain eye contact until the other person looks away. It might seem a bit strange at the beginning, but the more you practice, the more you'll build a habit of maintaining natural eye contact throughout the majority of the conversation. Only look away and break contact for purposes of thinking about what the other person is saying, pointing to an item used in the conversation, or taking a pause when speaking. These little natural breaks will help the eye contact stay consistent but not creepy.

3. *Stand your ground.* The art of assertiveness and charisma is all about making your presence known. For this, you'll have to learn a little bit about maintaining your territory, which subtly yet effectively signals personal power. You will start by taking slightly more space as you walk. Observe your stance as you walk the streets or enter a room. Do you shrug your shoulders and bow your head, mentally trying to make yourself invisible? Not anymore. Lift your head, straighten your shoulders, and spread your arms as much as possible while walking to feel more powerful but still natural. If you want to measure the ideal position, have your hands parallel with your shoulders, a few inches from your thighs, but with the elbows pointed outwards. As you walk, let your left-hand wave forward with the right leg and the other way around. This type of walk will help you feel and come across as stronger.

4. Set your boundaries. Boundaries are difficult for many people, but most notable at work. This is because the workplace is an environment with more people to push them. While some people are good at setting boundaries at work, many are less successful in personal life, where they can't say no to friends and family. Either way, setting boundaries requires making it clear what you will and will not tolerate. Your job is to sit down and review what you won't tolerate from people around you. Determining your boundaries means deciding what's acceptable and what's not, and it's okay to have different standards for home and work, as well as for different people. Now, to practice setting boundaries, you also need to start making them clear. Learn how to voice your boundaries assertively. Make sure that your response is balanced with the situation and that you're stating a clear message without overreacting.

Influencing Strangers

To influence a stranger—even if it's someone who might think they don't like us—we need to include another person in the mix. This person should be someone who's completely infatuated with you or, at least, likes and respects you. This other person must also be friendly with the stranger we're trying to influence. People tend to fall prey to herd mentality and jump on bandwagons. So, when the person who doesn't know you sees this other person gushing over you, it gives you an upper hand.

CONCLUSION

A person who captivates other people along his journey is someone who's known as charismatic and magnetic. They're like a magician that can talk to anyone, walk with anyone, influence anyone, and is liked by almost everyone. They're popular in every circle and are sought out by everyone because they're good company and fun to be around. They're the life of every party and steal the show effortlessly. Everyone wants to be around them, and their popularity grows every day.

If you want to be such a person, you need to put in time

and do the work. You need to start being more outgoing and extroverted. You need to interact with new people and put yourself out there by having new experiences. You need to learn how to make first impressions that leave people wanting to know more. They'll be unknowingly drawn to you after meeting you because your confidence and positivity are something they just can't fathom. Your confidence should shatter glass ceilings and glass walls. It should put you in charge of any situation without you ever having to say your name. Such a pinnacle of confidence can only be achieved by cultivating a positive self-image, which comes from self-love and healthy self-esteem.

So, while you're on this journey to be more charismatic and become the better version of yourself, truly personify the qualities of a healthy person: Someone who changes his old habits to make space for new ones. Someone who engages in positive self-talk and takes time to rejuvenate his body, soul, and mind.

That being said, there's more to a charismatic person than confidence. It's the ability to initiate small talk; exhibit impeccable facial, hand, and body gestures;

maintain eye contact; and attain an assertive position. It's the skill of dressing the part and effortlessly persuading anyone.

Now, the question is, what's stopping you from being the most charismatic version of yourself? Start today by paying heed to those around you and putting yourself out there. Start showing interest in people so you can truly be liked. Be sincere and respect other people's opinions. Make them feel important and encourage them to be themselves.

I hope that, through this book, you're able to learn how to put yourself out there, escape your social anxiety, and make some deep social connections. We've discussed a wide array of techniques, so choose a few to practice every week. Then, choose a few more and incorporate them, too. Keep practicing, and don't give up.

Be strong in your resolve. The outcome may be something you've never dreamed of. The validation you'll get from your peers will be worth it. The growth and maturity you'll sense in your personality will make this struggle worthwhile.

None of us is perfect. We'll always make mistakes and mess up. But, once you have confidence, instead of beating yourself up, you'll pick yourself up, start again, and keep going. You might want to join a support group. Support groups are cohorts of like-minded individuals that work together to achieve the same goal. When you work with people who are also determined to achieve the same goal, you'll find motivation in their struggle to keep going.

You can exchange tips and tricks to help each other and support each other when the road gets tough. You can learn from the mistakes of others and make this journey as fulfilling and as beneficial as possible. You can ask your friends and family to hold you accountable if you find ways to escape social gatherings or return to your old habits. You can make use of digital applications to set reminders for yourself and to motivate you to push on. Keep reminding yourself why you're doing this, what your objective is, and what's at stake. No one said this was going to be easy. If it was easy, everyone would be charismatic.

Being a magnetic and charismatic person who has the power of influence comes with practice, experience, and the will to change ourselves. If you read this book, it means you already have the drive to change yourself to become more charismatic. The only thing you need is commitment, hard work, and dedication, and you'll be successful in your endeavor in no time.

Thank you for reading this book, and good luck!

One More Thing!

If you enjoyed this book and found it helpful, I'd be very grateful if you'd post a short review on Amazon. Your support does make a difference, and I read all the reviews personally so I can get your feedback and make this book even better. I love hearing from my readers, and I'd really appreciate it if you leave your honest feedback.

Thank you for reading!

BONUS CHAPTER

I would like to share a sneak peek into another one of my books that I think you will enjoy. The book is titled _**" How to be Charismatic, Develop Confidence, and Exude Leadership: The Miracle Formula for Magnetic Charisma, Defeating Anxiety, and Winning at Communication"**_

This book will show you how to become a charismatic leader, develop sharp social skills, and become a passionate extrovert so that you can skyrocket your career, have healthier relationships, and grow genuine confidence and self-esteem!

119

But what if you're shy, introverted, and insecure? What if you feel like you don't have what it takes to grow and conquer your deepest dreams and desires? Don't worry! The simple tools you can learn right now are only a few clicks away!

The tips, tricks, and exercises given in this book will make you more attractive to anyone who meets you, including friends, coworkers, bosses, and romantic interests! This book will teach you how to:

- Discover and grow genuine charisma and magnetic appeal by tapping into your inner goodness, beauty, and passion to motivate yourself and others
- Start developing social skills to make new acquaintances, spread your influence, and increase personal power
- Nurture deep, meaningful, healthy, and mutually supportive relationships
- Build true, unshakeable confidence by nurturing your authenticity and self-esteem

- Become an effective listener to establish deep connections and detect people's needs, desires, and motives
- Convey and read body language to exude confidence, positivity, and strength
- Click with people around you to compel them with your magnetic charisma
- Increase your popularity and extend your social network
- Grow a leader's confidence and mindset by setting goals, contributing to the group, and motivating and supporting others
- Leave a positive, memorable first impression by making others feel comfortable, heard, and important
- Develop leadership communication skills, such as listening, interacting with individuals and groups, telling stories, and resolving conflicts
- Develop presence and magnetism to attract people all around, spread your message with passion and clarity, and

grow talent to persuade people into doing what you want

- Practice an assertive attitude so that you can stop being shy, learn to say no, stand up for yourself without being aggressive, and set healthy boundaries that honor you and the people around you

Hop on a train toward the discovery of your hidden charisma, strengths, and potentials. This book shows you how to leverage simple, affordable, and accessible resources like knowledge and your own inborn talents to find your authentic self and showcase it to the world. No more hiding! The world deserves to see you! Start your journey right now and notice how you're becoming more socially competent and confident on the very same day!

Enjoy this free chapter!

Do you want to become the best version of yourself? Do you want to become memorable, appeal to people, and find personal and business success? Do you want to overcome shyness and insecurity and become more authentic and popular?

If you want all these things, it means that you have everything it takes to become a charismatic leader, and this book will show you exactly how to do that! *How to be Charismatic, Develop Confidence, and Exude Leadership: The Miracle Formula for Magnetic Charisma, Defeating Anxiety, and Winning at Communication* will help you get from where you are now to where you want to be by developing ten crucial leadership skills!

This book is for everyone looking to develop social skills, establish deep relationships, open themselves up to the world, and attract people with their bulletproof confidence and intoxicating charisma. Don't believe this can be you? Just wait!

This book will show you the exact techniques and give you the right tools to find the deeply hidden seed of charisma and grow it until it bursts and shines through you in a blinding, jaw-dropping aura that attracts people like moths are drawn to a flame.

How will this book do this for you? It's quite simple. This book will teach you all about charisma and magnetic appeal that you can start nurturing and growing today on any budget just by reaching deep down into the most beautiful depths of your inner being. This book will show you how to find and grab your positive values, strengths, and talents and make them your trademark.

Upon learning how to harvest the fruits of charisma, you'll learn how to develop social skills needed to extend your network of acquaintances, enrich your relationships, upscale your career, and influence people to get what you want. This book will show you how to become an active, engaged, and empathetic listener who makes a killer first impression and leaves people hungry for your presence.

To do this, you will find out how to get people to like you, and it will not be by putting on a mask. No! You will learn how to showcase your authentic self with the way you dress, speak, and shake hands so that everyone who meets you gets to know and love what they see. If you follow the instructions given in this book, you'll be able to show others the genuine, strong, and confident you. You will know how to appeal to people's hidden motivations and desires and connect with what you have in common.

Once you learn how to get people to like you, this book will show you how to form better and deeper relationships. You'll learn how to master the art of small talk to set the basis for deeper relationships and leverage these connections to give and take for the sake of mutual progress.

That's right! This book will show you how to become an altruistic, inspiring, and charismatic leader who wears their life's true purpose like one wears a suit and helps other people achieve their goals.

In this book, you will also find out how to become more assertive so that you can balance your feelings and attitude for more productive work and personal relationships. Aren't you tired of being shy and hiding in your cocoon? No more saying yes to things you don't want and doing things that step on your dignity and self-esteem just to please people! In this book, you will learn how to set healthy boundaries so that you can show people what they can and cannot do and what you are and aren't willing to tolerate. More importantly, you'll learn how to do this in a calm, respectful way—that is, respectful both to you and the people around you.

That's right! Assertiveness skills explained in this book will show you how to stand up for yourself without hostility and conflict. Isn't that amazing?

But how do you get there? How do you appeal to people to that extent if you're introverted and shy? What do you do if merely talking to people frightens you? Don't worry—you're covered!

This book will give you the basic knowledge for growing and nurturing true confidence and self-esteem based on your authentic personality and best traits. In this book, you'll learn how true confidence looks and how to start practicing it so that you know and understand that you're an infinitely worthy person who can rely on their talents and skills to advance in life. You will learn simple everyday techniques and tips to apply to feel better about yourself and truly believe in your own worth. But that's not all!

This book will tear the misconception that loving yourself means being selfish, and it will show you how to be respectful, truthful, and empathetic. Aside from learning how to become a leader, you will learn how to become a leader who gives and contributes to their group or organization. You will learn how to share ideas and feedback that build everyone up so that you and the people around you are successfully working toward a common goal.

This book will also show you how to use the best of your abilities to observe and read people, as well as use your appearance, performance, and body language to speak and spread your authentic message. Following the principles and instructions given in this book will help you trade the best of your strengths for respect and popularity with your friends, coworkers, and family. Simply put, this book will show you how to reach into the best you have and share it with the world, and then you will receive the sweet fruits of your charismatic labor.

Don't wait another minute! Your hidden potentials, core values, and infinite strengths are waiting to be discovered, grown, and plucked to bring you love, acceptance, and success you so deeply desire. With each minute that passes, your potentials are being wasted on self-defeating thoughts and self-sabotaging behaviors, and you are losing time and money on doing things for other people just because you're unable to say no!

Hurry up and start learning to make a great first impression. At the beginning of this book, you'll find out what you can do today so that people remember you and want to connect with you. Aren't you excited to lead?

What if I told you that how you come across during the first 30 seconds of meeting new people affects nearly 85 percent of your business success? What if I told you that the person you like takes only a split second to decide whether they like you or not. Doesn't it sound scary? That's because it is! Just imagine. Out of thousands of hours spent learning and doing hard work to build your career, mornings and evenings spent working out to get yourself in shape, all the planning that goes into your career, or all the charity work you do to make the world a better place, those initial 30 seconds determine the majority of your success!

If you still haven't freaked out, just wait. Remember the last time you made a new acquaintance. Maybe it was a bank clerk, a possible network connection, or your friend's friend who works for a major brand. It could even be your neighbor's coworker, who has a gorgeous son or daughter right about your age. What did these encounters look like? What did you say? How did you look? Were you clean and polished, or were you dressed in rags because you were cleaning your backyard?

How you carry yourself and act around other people determines your success regardless of your true skills, talents, and positive traits. Nailing that first impression can open many doors, point out shortcuts, and help you make long-term connections. But how do you do that? How do you make people remember you and want to talk to you in less than a minute? Lucky for you, you've come to the right place to get your answer.

Right before we get into the strategies for making an awesome first impression, let's briefly address why this is a challenge in the first place. When you're about to meet someone new, your fight-or-flight response gets triggered. Your unconscious brain evaluates whether or not you feel safe around the particular person, and it is particularly keen on detecting anything that's potentially threatening. If you look into the dynamic of first encounters, the truth is that it includes two or more people who instantly start deciding whether the new person seems safe to be around or they're to be avoided. Now, the way this works is that your unconscious mind detects the general appearance, body language, and other peculiarities regarding the other person and makes conclusions based on that. The same goes for those who evaluate you. The best way to make a great first impression is to send out more "green flags" than "red flags." This means to dress and behave in ways that help people feel safe and eliminate those behaviors that, unconsciously, signal danger.

Having a positive attitude means allowing the best of you to shine through your attitude and conversations. However, this positivity needs to be genuine and not imposed (i.e., toxic positivity). It's important to remember to consistently work on how you see the world so that you're able to maintain a positive, optimistic outlook on a situation while acknowledging the present reality. A general rule might be that people prefer positive people. However, if your job is to market yourself as a grief consultant, to say that you should act punchy and upbeat would be wrong. In this situation, you should level your mindset to be empathetic with the people you talk to, but be positive-oriented in the way you send your messages and talk to them. When talking to people in a business setting or at a party, it would be appropriate to show your most confident, upbeat self. What do you do when that's inappropriate? Then you adjust to how you can make the situation better.

Toxic positivity, on the other hand, is present in people we perceive as disingenuous. These people make false claims and statements of not only their success but also what others can do. Their intentions are self-involved, and that's easy to notice. They can only fool those who are emotionally and mentally vulnerable—and even that is only temporary. So when speaking about positivity, keep in mind that I'm referring to a genuinely helpful, optimistic attitude in your appearance and mannerisms aimed at making everyone around you feel a bit better than they felt before they met you. At times, you will do this using jokes, and other times, it will be through consolation and the words of support.

Get your full copy today! *__"How to be Charismatic, Develop Confidence, and Exude Leadership: The Miracle Formula for Magnetic Charisma, Defeating Anxiety, and Winning at Communication"__*

BOOKS BY RICHARD BANKS

How to be Charismatic, Develop Confidence, and Exude Leadership: The Miracle Formula for Magnetic Charisma, Defeating Anxiety, and Winning at Communication

How to Stop Being Negative, Angry, and Mean: Master Your Mind and Take Control of Your Life

How to Deal with Grief, Loss, and Death: A Survivor's Guide to Coping with Pain and Trauma, and Learning to Live Again

How to Deal With Stress, Depression, and Anxiety: A Vital Guide on How to Deal with Nerves and Coping with Stress, Pain, OCD and Trauma

The Positive Guide to Anger Management: The Most Practical Guide on How to Be Calmer, Learn to Defeat Anger, Deal with Angry People, and Living a Life of

Mental Wellness and Positivity

Develop a Positive Mindset and Attract the Life of Your Dreams: Unleash Positive Thinking to Achieve Unbound Happiness, Health, and Success

The Keys to Being Brilliantly Confident and More Assertive: A Vital Guide to Enhancing Your Communication Skills, Getting Rid of Anxiety, and Building Assertiveness

Personal Development Mastery 2 Books in 1: The Keys to being Brilliantly Confident and More Assertive + How to be Charismatic, Develop Confidence, and Exude Leadership

Positive Mindset Mastery 2 Books in 1: Develop a Positive Mindset and Attract the Life of Your Dreams + How to Stop Being Negative, Angry, and Mean